Helicopters

Experts on child reading levels
have consulted on the level of text and
concepts in this book.

At the end of the book is a "Look Back and Find" section
which provides additional information and encourages
the child to refer back to previous pages
for the answers to the questions posed.

Angela Grunsell trained as a teacher in 1969.
She has a Diploma in Reading and Related Skills
and for the last five years has advised London
teachers on materials and resources.

Published in the United States in 1987 by
Franklin Watts, 387 Park Avenue South, New York, NY 10016

© Aladdin Books Ltd/Franklin Watts

Designed and produced by
Aladdin Books Ltd, 70 Old Compton Street, London W1

ISBN 0-531-10284-X
Library of Congress
Catalog Card Number: 86-50803
Printed in Belgium

FRANKLIN · WATTS · FIRST · LIBRARY

Helicopters

by
Kate Petty

Consultant
Angela Grunsell

Illustrated by
Douglas Harker

Franklin Watts
New York · London · Toronto · Sydney

What can helicopters do?
They can go straight up and straight down.
They can go backward and sideways.
They can hover and they can lift things.

Beta R22

MIL Mi-10 Harke

Helicopters are very useful aircraft.
The little crop-sprayer can fly slowly and
close to the ground. The enormous skycrane
is big enough to help you move home!

When the rotor blades whirl around, the helicopter lifts off the ground. It usually flies at 2,300 to 3,300 feet. The tail rotor stops the helicopter itself from spinning.

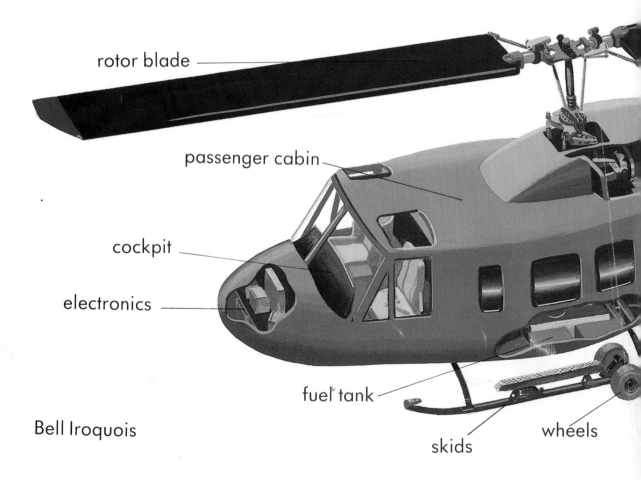

rotor blade

passenger cabin

cockpit

electronics

fuel tank

skids

wheels

Bell Iroquois

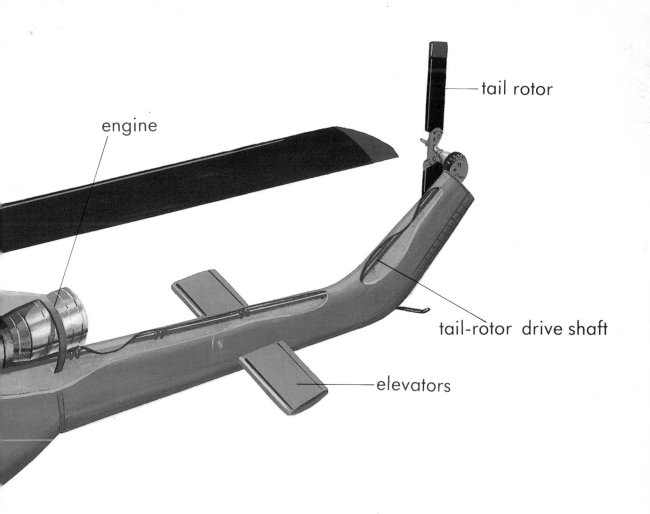

engine

tail rotor

tail-rotor drive shaft

elevators

The powerful engine, which drives the
rotors, uses a fuel called kerosene.
This helicopter can fly as fast as 200 mph.
It has wheels as well as skids to land on.

MBB BO 106

For a helicopter to fly, the upward push of the air must be stronger than the downward push. The spinning rotor blades are shaped to break up the airflow and make this happen.

It takes a lot of practice to learn how to
control an aircraft which can do
so many things. Pilots first learn to
fly an airplane that has "fixed wings."

Unlike an airport, a heliport can be right in a city, because helicopters need very little space to take off and land. They can even land on the roofs of tall buildings.

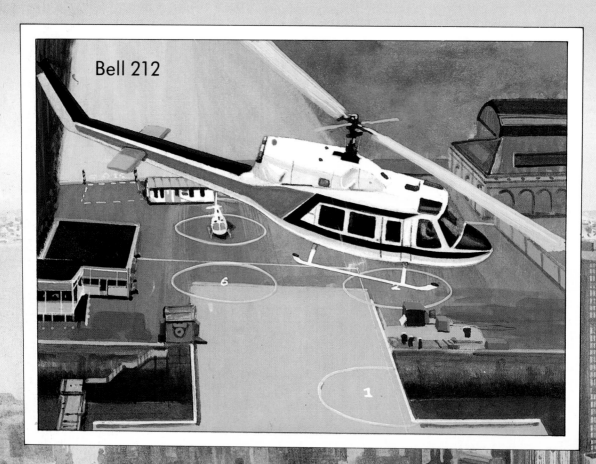

Bell 212

This helicopter carries nine people.
The passengers are usually
business executives or politicians
who need to be in a place quickly.

Bell 222

Bell 222

Why do you think the police find
helicopters useful? They can get
a good view of traffic building up
or of a crowd getting out of control.

14

With heli-tele they can relay instant pictures of a bank robbery to police on the ground. At speeds over 150 mph they also have a good chance of catching up with a getaway car.

Bell 212 rescue helicopter

If people fall overboard in stormy seas,
rescue by helicopter may be their only hope.
Rescue helicopters like this one have a
computerized system to help them spot survivors.

16

The latest rescue helicopter can stay on auto-hover while the winch is fixed to the injured person. It also has infrared "sight" so the rescue work can go on after dark.

Oil rigs are nearly always in places which are difficult to get to, whether they are in the middle of a jungle, a desert, or far out to sea. Helicopters are their lifeline.

Helicopters carry the crew to and from the rig, bring in supplies and take people to a hospital if they are sick. High winds and fog can make landing on the heli-deck a difficult job.

Aerospatiale 330 Puma

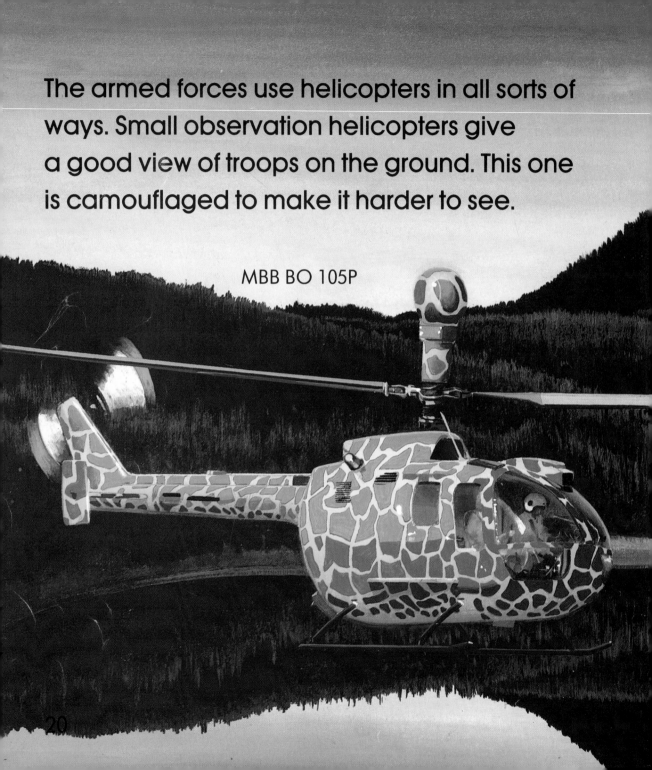

The armed forces use helicopters in all sorts of ways. Small observation helicopters give a good view of troops on the ground. This one is camouflaged to make it harder to see.

MBB BO 105P

Boeing Chinook

Helicopters can quickly transport soldiers and equipment right to where they are needed. The twin-rotor Chinook is strong enough to carry heavy vehicles and weapons.

Attack helicopters are the gunships of the air. Armed with a gun underneath and missiles below the wing stubs, they can help out troops and tanks on the ground.

Helicopters are fast and dangerous in battle, for the 2-man crew as well as their targets. The pilot usually sits behind and above the observer/gunner.

A129 Mongoose Agusta

MIL Mi-24 Hind

This naval helicopter is trying to pick up
sounds from a hidden submarine.
It is dipping a buoy which contains
sonar equipment into the sea.

Westland Sea King

There are helicopters as well as fighter jets on an aircraft carrier. In a battle at sea Sea Lynxes would be used to attack ships and submarines with missiles.

Westland/Aerospatiale Sea Lynx

The basic shape of helicopters has hardly changed in the fifty years they have been flying. They are still quite slow compared with other aircraft.

Hughes LHX

The X-wing is a design for a future helicopter.
The four rotor blades could become two pairs
of fixed wings for faster flight. The helicopter
would then become an airplane!

Look back and find

What is this helicopter doing?

Why is a helicopter useful for this job?

What other jobs might farmers
use helicopters for?

What does the pilot do to the rotor blades
to alter the course of the helicopter?
*The blades can be twisted for climbing
and turning. They are all tilted together
for forward and backward flight.*

Why should it be more expensive to
fly in a helicopter than an airliner?
Helicopters carry fewer people.

Why can a helicopter land and take off
in a small space?

Why are helicopters so useful for rescue at sea?
Rough seas are dangerous for lifeboats. A helicopter can hover above the waves to search for someone and winch them to safety.

What is special about infrared "sight"?

Why is this helicopter painted?

How could you guess that it is an observation helicopter?

Who else might use an observation helicopter?

Which is faster, a fixed-wing aircraft or a helicopter?

How could a helicopter be turned into a fixed-wing aircraft?

What is this one called?

Index